Dedicating this book, and all that I do,
to my wildlife warrior parents, brother,
husband, and beautiful daughter.
You are my reason for being.
—B.I.

For my wonderful boys, Gabriel, Rafi & Tom,
and all wildlife warriors big and small
—S.P.-H.

For my beautiful niece, Eleonora
—R.K.

Text copyright © 2025 by Australia Zoo Productions
Jacket art and interior illustrations copyright © 2025 by Ramona Kaulitzki
Photographs courtesy of Kate Berry and Australia Zoo

All rights reserved. Published in the United States by Random House Children's Books,
a division of Penguin Random House LLC, 1745 Broadway, New York, NY 10019.

Random House and the colophon are registered trademarks of Penguin Random House LLC.

Visit us on the Web! rhcbooks.com
Educators and librarians, for a variety of teaching tools, visit us at RHTeachersLibrarians.com

Library of Congress Cataloging-in-Publication Data is available upon request.
ISBN 978-0-593-42811-5 (trade) — ISBN 978-0-593-42812-2 (lib. bdg.) — ISBN 978-0-593-42813-9 (ebook)

The artist used Adobe Photoshop and watercolor to create the illustrations for this book.
The text is set in 16-point Isidora Sans.
Interior design by Elizabeth Tardiff

MANUFACTURED IN CHINA
10 9 8 7 6 5 4 3 2 1
First Edition

Random House Children's Books supports the First Amendment and celebrates the right to read.

Penguin Random House LLC supports copyright. Copyright fuels creativity, encourages diverse voices,
promotes free speech, and creates a vibrant culture. Thank you for buying an authorized edition of this book and
for complying with copyright laws by not reproducing, scanning, or distributing any part in any form without permission.
You are supporting writers and allowing Penguin Random House to publish books for every reader.

You Are a Wildlife Warrior!

Saving Animals & the Planet

by Bindi Irwin

with Smriti Prasadam-Halls

illustrated by Ramona Kaulitzki

Random House 🏠 New York

G'day. It's so lovely that you're here. Thank you for picking up my book and embarking on this special adventure with me and my beautiful daughter, Grace.

My hope is that this book will help to inspire the next generation of change-makers to love, respect, and protect our natural world. I want to encourage more kids to understand that we are all connected and we can show kindness toward Mother Earth on a daily basis.

My dad first created the term *wildlife warrior* many years ago to describe us and the work we do as a family. To be a wildlife warrior means to stand up and speak for those who cannot speak for themselves.

In our work as wildlife warriors, conservation through exciting education is our ethos. We support projects around the world protecting wildlife.

It is an honor to tell our family story in this book, sharing an inside look at our lives as conservationists. My daughter is growing up surrounded by Australia Zoo's gorgeous gardens, its spectacular wildlife, and our extended zoo family, who all work together to protect the planet and educate others. I can see the kindness Grace already shows to animals, and it warms my heart. I'm thankful that I get to continue with our wildlife warrior work and have her along for the journey with me.

As a mother, it's more important to me than ever to reach out to the next generations and spark love and empathy toward all living things.

Love, Bindi

When you're a wildlife warrior,
the world feels big and new.
Each day's a fresh adventure—
waiting just for you!

We care for animals in the zoo.
Our hearts beat for conservation.
Through our work out in the wild,
we protect the next generation.

By paying close attention,
we learn each creature's ways.
We learn about their habitats
and how they spend their days.

We are wildlife warriors—
watching over one and all.
We care for those with fur . . .

. . . or scales.

DID YOU KNOW?

Koalas will sleep for up to 20 hours every day!

Giant tortoises can live more than 100 years!

We love them big!

DID YOU KNOW?

Giraffes have long necks to help them eat leaves from the tallest of trees.

White rhinos—which are not actually white—have two horns and square lips!

DID YOU KNOW?

A baby echidna is called a puggle!

Ring-tailed lemurs live in social groups called troops, which are ruled by one female.

We love them small!

DID YOU KNOW?

Red pandas wrap their long, bushy tail around their body to keep warm in cold weather.

Meerkats have sharp claws for digging burrows, which help them stay cool in the heat.

We are wildlife warriors.
We observe how babies grow.
They change and they flourish,
learning what they need to know.

DID YOU KNOW?

There are over 850 species of birds native to Australia!

Those babies get so strong and sure.
They strut and hop and bounce.
We see them gain the confidence
to jump and fly and flounce!

Wildlife warriors learn to treasure
each diverse environment on earth.
Deserts, forests, oceans, jungles:
we know their meaning and their worth.

Wherever we do our conservation,
we work to nurture and protect.
And at the zoo's wildlife hospital,
we treat animals with kindness and respect.

DID YOU KNOW?

The Australia Zoo Wildlife Hospital treats over 10,000 animals per year.

It has had over 11,000 koalas admitted since 2004.

Learning, conserving, observing:
wildlife warriors do it all!
So come along on our mission—
answer the wildlife call!

Since I can remember, my parents always encouraged my love for wildlife and wild places.

They brought me and my brother along for all their conservation missions. I will always be thankful that they chose to involve us in their mission to make the world a better place. One of my earliest memories takes place in the ocean. Mum and Dad were filming a conservation documentary along the coast of Western Australia. We were in the ocean together, and I was holding on to my dad's shoulders with my little water wings on my arms. Suddenly, a pod of wild dolphins approached us and started jumping over our heads as the sun was setting. It was one of the most moving and memorable experiences of my life, which I will treasure forever. I've always known that I wanted to follow in my parents' footsteps, protecting the natural world.

Now, as a mother, I want to do the same for my daughter, Grace. To give her the opportunity to follow her dreams and enjoy this extraordinary planet we call home.

Our family lives in and owns the conservation sanctuary Australia Zoo. We strive to create remarkable habitats for our animal family and the world's best experiences for our guests. At Australia Zoo, we have an incredible team of over four hundred, who work to educate and inspire our guests to appreciate the natural world. We have vital breeding programs for endangered species, daily educational talks, school groups, tours, volunteer initiatives, and a passion to bring exciting education to everyone who visits. Our grounds feature spacious safe havens for our animals, with thousands of native flora species.

We also run the nonprofit organization Wildlife Warriors, which supports conservation projects around the world.

In Africa we work with three organizations:

The Black Mambas, an all-female, army-trained anti-poaching team within the Olifants West Nature Reserve in South Africa.

Ol Pejeta Conservancy, protecting the critically endangered black rhinos, with specially trained K-9 Units working alongside the rangers.

Cheetah Outreach's Livestock Guarding Dog Program, which places Anatolian shepherd dogs with herds of livestock to deter predators—saving cheetahs from being shot by farmers.

In Sumatra we have two very important projects with tigers and elephants. We help to employ full-time forest rangers who patrol the jungle and dismantle illegal tiger snare traps.

Our Australia Zoo Wildlife Hospital and Rescue Unit treats about 10,000 patients per year and continues to expand, utilizing cutting-edge medical treatments for the wildlife that comes into our care. Our philosophy is "save one, save the species." The goal with every animal is to give them the best chance at life in the wild once again. It's humbling to know that with so many animals treated, we are helping to save entire species. We have the most dedicated team, who pour everything they have into saving the lives of wild animals that come to our hospital.

It's heartwarming to see the younger generation getting involved with conservation initiatives. Our nonprofit organization has a component called Visionary Wildlife Warriors, encouraging kids under eighteen to get involved with creating positive change on the planet. From conservation missions to wildlife protection fundraising, this program gives kids the platform and ability to be the change within their community and beyond. I've seen firsthand the extraordinary response from kids wanting to make the world a better place.

The great thing is, you don't have to be a conservationist to have compassion for the living beings we share the earth with. The littlest of things can make a big difference for our planet. Invest in a reusable water bottle, recycle, plant a tree, start an insect or bird garden in your backyard, turn off the tap when you brush your teeth, volunteer at a wildlife organization in your area, take part in a beach or park cleanup day, never purchase any products made from wild animals. These thoughtful acts all add up to become enormous strides toward protecting our environment.

Believe in your strength to make a huge impact, and never underestimate the power of a kind gesture. That kindness can change the world.